Once upon a time,

there was a boy named Barnaby.

He lived with his mother and father

in a small house by a brook.

Barnaby was a good boy.
Every day he helped his mother
in the garden and fed the chickens.

Barnaby's father was the king's cook.
Every day he would cross the brook,
walk into the woods, and go up to the castle.
There he would cook fine meals for the king.

One day Barnaby's father left home in a hurry.
The king had asked a good friend to lunch.
The friend loved fresh jam cakes,
and jam cakes took a lot of time to make.

After he had gone,

Barnaby saw his father's cookbook on the shelf.

"Look!" Barnaby said.

"Father left this important book.

He needs it to cook his jam cakes!"

"Run and take it to him!" said Barnaby's mother.

"Hurry! Take your hood. It's cold out!"

Barnaby put on his hood.

He took the book, ran to the brook,

and jumped over on the stones.

Then he ran down the path into the woods.

It was a cold day.

The wind shook the trees.

Barnaby shook under his hood,

but he did not stop.

He had to get the cookbook to his father.

He ran out of the woods
and into the big castle.
He saw many people,
but where was his father?

Barnaby looked up and down.

He looked here and there.

Where could his father be?

At last he sat down to think.

"My father is the king's cook," he said.

"Where would I look for a cook?"

Just then Barnaby's nose began to twitch.

He could smell something—

something good.

He followed the smell, and . . .

. . . there was his father, baking cookies!

His father took the cookbook
and gave Barnaby a big hug.
"Thank you, Barnaby," he said.
"I needed this cookbook.
Why don't you stay here today
and help me cook?
I will send a note to your mother,
so she will not look for you."

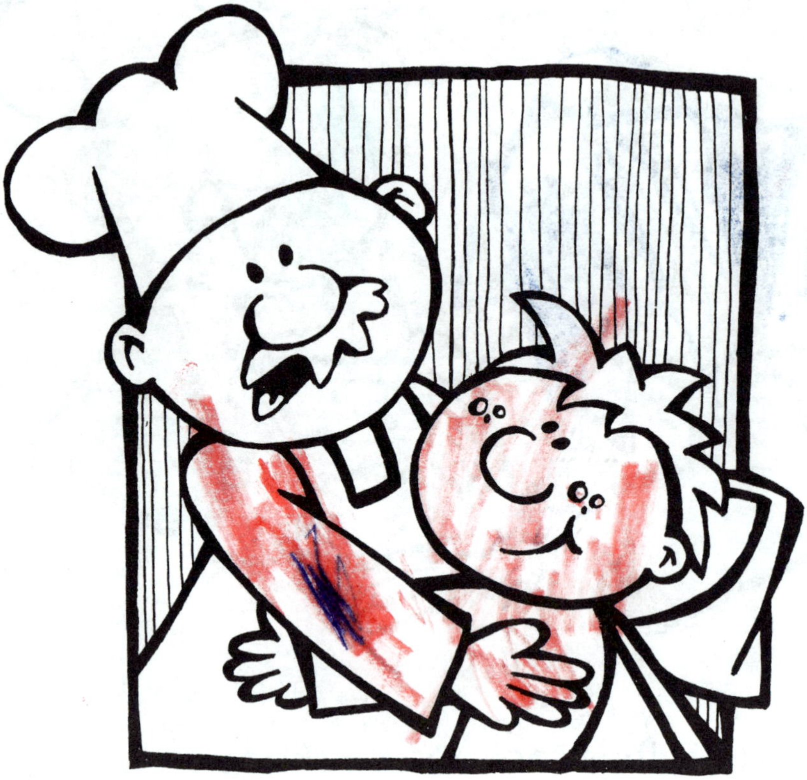

Barnaby hugged his father.
He felt very happy
and very important.